Here Co
the Shapes

Story by Jenny Giles

Illustrations by Boris Silvestri

"I am not going
to go to sleep,"
said Little Red.
"I am going to go down
into the garden."

"Wake up, Little Blue,"
said Little Red.
"I am going down into the garden.
Come on. You come, too!"

Little Red and Little Blue
went down into the garden.

Little Red went on the swing.

Little Blue went on the slide.

"Look!" said Little Blue.
"I can see Mum and Dad.
They are going up to bed!"

"Come on! Run!"
said Little Red.

Little Red and Little Blue ran back to bed.

"Look," said Mum.

"Little Blue is asleep."

“Look,” said Dad.

“Little Red is asleep.”

1, 2, 3.
Look at me.
4, 5, 6.
Up to tricks.